From *the* *Insights* *Series*

Insights **A** Shy
From **A** Entrepreneur
▫

Grazing **Minds**
Publishing

Turning Slowdown
into
Opportunity

Book - 2

Of a 3 book series on frugal
entrepreneurship essentials

By:

DASH
ASISH

Table of Contents

Insights From
A Shy
Entrepreneur

INSIGHTS FROM
A SHY
ENTREPRENEUR

Turning Slowdown
Into
Opportunity
Volume : 2

ASISH DASH

A GRAZING MINDS BOOK

PAGE INTENTIONALLY left blank

Grazing Minds Publishing,
Grazing Minds Research And Consulting LLP
Parinee Crescenzo, G Block,
BKC, Bandra East,
Mumbai, Maharashtra - 400051
INDIA
Email: sayhello@grazingminds.co.in

Grazing Minds and the GM logo are registered trademarks of Grazing Minds Research and Consulting LLP.

This second iteration of the book is dedicated to my readers, whose immense support and adulation received from the first book's success propelled me to write another one!!

Also, I would like to dedicate this book to all those souls – who left us during this Covid period : like my grandfather!!
Someone who always cherished my success, but never admired me infront of me – but always held pride in me, behind my back!!

That's how elders are!!!

I am thankful to my dear mom & dad, who have been inspiring me and have stood by me during my numerous ventures.

Page intentionally left blank

Preface

With the previous book in the series: Insight from a Shy Entrepreneur, Volume 1: Turning Common Traits into Rare Skillsets, we touched upon few aspects of skill-building. We discussed about the kind of thinking it takes to become one entrepreneur.

Between the first book and now a lot has changed.

Our economy has exploded with entrepreneurs and there has been shrinkage in the funds. The initial euphoria of having a startup – where you were slush with funds and growth at all costs was the norm, has changed now to sustainable business practices, where reality has dawned upon enterprises. In the new world order, If I may – the earlier gamble is withering off.

Now, it's no longer sufficient to just have a business idea – where you go about creating MVP or validating it after raising your pre-seed or seed round.

Today vanity metrics don't matter, because ultimately the customer won't give a damn about your metrics. Sustainability and Profitability is the key today.

This requires a change in mindset of everyone – especially the business community to succeed. In this book we will discuss about tools, new mindsets, and key decisions which will help us cross the tide of slowdown or funding crunch and help us make decisions which will make your business last atleast a few more years and help fight the new world order.

Page intentionally left blank

Prelude - As you may term it

Okay, before we get started with the book chapters,

Here is something for my readers

In their

20s

30s

40s

50s

Or

Should i Say X's

There's so much "advice" for X-year-olds & I'm gonna call it out.

10 things to do in your Xs.

5 Books you MUST read in your Xs.

3 Habits to develop in your Xs.

Oh my good lord, please stop!

Look, I'm about 34'ish someone. I know many people in their 20s, 30s and 40s.

Everyone's working hard, relentlessly pursuing what they love & have a passion for.

Some are doing it with their full-time jobs (most of them don't like it).

But then come these pieces of advice

&

I honestly just skip through

Because
those people upload it every second day.
I'm sorry but the average X-year-old you're targeting,
is still reading the books from your first video,
because they're shit scared
Of
"If I don't read this book on entrepreneurship, I'll lose".
Here's what I've told myself:
"It's okay if you don't know the ABCs of crypto dude.
It's fine if you haven't read Zero to One so far.
You'll do that but it's not a race of- "Who finished reading all "the"
books
Or
inculcated all "the" habits."
If that's a race at all, count me out.
People have missed out on so much perspective.
Do you think FOMO's going to get you to take action?
Nope.
There has to be a balance.
Dear X something's, slow down.
Slowing down doesn't mean what you think it does.
Guess, now you all are lil eased up as I wanted to throw your stress/
eagerness out of the window/door before we start out!
As the old adage goes,
One cannot learn, what you think you already know!!
If you already know, you have lost out on time,age,opportunities
Your mind will always be stuck on that
And
Change cannot happen!!!
Why listen to me?

Well, this comes from someone
Who failed in a English test when he was 10 years old
But
Topped National English Lit. Exam when tides turned to 17 years
And
Still is able to write books - one or two!!!
Or
Someone who lost in business,
Because the main vendor bailed out,
Because the partner pursued own interests and never took the main
business seriously
But
Was able to
Start businesses from scratch -
Which later attracted VC's and PE's !!
So bottomline: Don't be bogged down by your failure or missed op-
portunities.
Till we are alive, we are full of possibilities....

So
Before dwelling further,
Please understand –
It's not easy to live your life,
You have to make it easy!
You may ask how?
Well - some part of it by Patience, Some by Tolerance
And a lot more by IGNORING !!
So don't ever think "My way is highway"
Be humble...

In My Opinion,
Humility is the strongest characteristic in any human being
So do remember, you can ease out your stress, your life – be it personal or professional,
By
Bit of patience, bit of tolerance and with a lot of IGNORING!!
AND SO,
With a clear head, let's get started!!
Page intentionally left blank

Chapter 1: Knowledge Grows Your Fear

Before you reach to some out of the way random conclusion, let's take a step back and think:

How many PhD scholars do you know who run successful enterprises?!?

And NO, I am not saying about those nerds running Hospitals or Pharma companies - But normal business.

Now, I know a lot of academic scholars are going to have negative impressions about me - But hey, don't get judgemental. I have something more for you (in a good sense) in the following chapters.

I don't know if you have observed or not, but I have learnt this the hard way that a highly learned man could be a dependent lieutenant in your entrepreneurship journey, but not your partner!!

Why?

Simple, because they know a lot more. The tons of in-depth knowledge they have prevents them from taking risks - because, in their head, they start calculating the probability of success and failure. And, in my honest view - an entrepreneurship effort by default starts with a high failure rate.

If you find a business that has a cent per cent success rate - what gets projected on your pitch gets exactly executed with the same success ratio - well then:

a) Everyone would be doing it

b) It sounds too good to be true but will most often than not, end you in some kind of trap - one where you will either lose money, name, fame or at least your valuable time.

Entrepreneurship is often venturing out into the unknown. On a superficial level, you may find all variables as known - in your control, but at a subdural level, there are many unknown variables on which the success of that venture depends.

Heck, the chances of a venture getting successful are almost equivalent to space programs of nations - Sometimes a hit and sometimes a big big Miss!!

So, How do you define "entrepreneur"?

My definition:

An individual—building a product or service—that has outsized control over their time and the trajectory of what they are building.

Now, sometimes we also come across the term entrepreneurial-mindset. There's a clear distinction between being an entrepreneur & having an entrepreneurial-mindset.

One is about having ownership over your time and future.

One is about having an owner's mentality.

Now I checked out what my dear friend "Google" defines as an entrepreneur!!

🔊 **en·tre·pre·neur**

/ˌäntrəprəˈnər, ˌäntrəprəˈno͞o(ə)r/

noun

a person who organizes and operates a business or businesses, taking on greater than normal financial risks in order to do so.

"many entrepreneurs see potential in this market"

Similar: businessman   businesswoman   ∨

The definition of entrepreneur is changing before our eyes. It's no longer about taking greater than normal financial risk.

Now let's get back to the topic of knowledge and entrepreneurship.

So in my opinion, the more you start getting knowledge on a topic - the more avenues you get to see for failure.

Interestingly enough, sometimes these events may not even occur for failure to happen in the real world - but what this extra knowledge does is - it creates a fear within you, which makes you cautious to an extent that you start finding negativity in the plan and always almost drop it!!!

Knowledge is essential no doubt, but there is no end to the knowledge in entrepreneurship. In business, knowledge is that "chain reaction" of which there can be various permutations and combinations, which cannot be "experimented" upon a closed or ideal condition.

Hence, in my opinion - to increase your probability of success, you just need to know the basics of "chain reaction" - keep some funds at disposable so you can procure additional resources whenever the need arises to keep your experiment in an "ideal environment" and also keep learning new trends to handle emergencies smartly!!

You see Colonel Sanders of KFC, never studied to become a Sous chef or the likes. He did plenty of odd jobs and found potential in a particular "void" and jumped in. Through experimentations - failures and hits, he found which style of cooking works and which spice mixture works for the audience. Had he got formal training, he would have been blinded by the boundaries of knowledge. There would be negligible or minimal urge to break those shackles.

Let's relate it to today's time.

With such rapid advancement of technology, you simply cannot limit yourself to traditional business theory.

Those that thought conventionally (quite a majority of the people) say for instance never believed in crypto-currency. Such was the fear of economists, that even Central Banks of countries banned it and even tried to influence banks to stop payments to any crypto trading platform. Well, that was a few years back and today, well its market value exceeds that of Alibaba!!

Those economists, if they could have invested $1000 in a currency - they so ridiculed, well - they could be vacationing the rest of their life in the Bahamas or Maldives.

But,

What happened?!?

Almost every senior economist, be it on the Boards of Central Banks, Researchers in prestigious universities, everyone denounced the "unknown"!!

I don't know the future of crypto, nor will I debate about it here. But all I wanted to concur was, if we take a "calculated" plunge/risk towards the "unknown" and work/learn on it, then the chances of success increases manifold!!!

The same goes with even Elon Musk.

Some brand him a "glorified failure", but today he has become the wealthiest man on the planet.

When other car manufacturers got themselves blinded by traditional gasoline-powered engines, someone had the vision and ability to change the game.

End result?

We all know that the market cap/valuation of major car manufacturers combined falls just short of that of TESLA.

So bottom line, a basic amount of knowledge is good - which helps set up and start the business. But post that, if you have an option to spend your time in growing your business or getting more degrees - well, my inclination will be towards business.

Here let me also say, learning for the growth of the business is a never-ending and continuous process.....

Say today you learnt about invoicing, then you have taxation, compliance, sometimes even becoming the hardware engineer with a crash course from Youtube...

So don't think, just because you don't have that PhD or degree from the Ivy League - you won't succeed!! - That's a big fallacy and a dampener to any soul's motivation.

So get it out with...

In industry, some people like Peter Thiel have said stuff against B school grad's like "Never hire an M.B.A.; they will ruin your company."

Well, it's partly true to an extent.

Your employees belonging to top schools, give you the bragging rights in front of your client's about the talent pool you hold and in return charge them a premium. However, if you are an innovation-driven organization or a startup with direct end usage products to customers, the alma mater of your employees makes a marginal difference.

Sometimes it is because you don't give responsibilities to someone in an organization which can make or break things - just because of academic excellence. Having learned from the best schools and institutions, I can say one thing with utmost confidence "Nothing you learnt in school will help you innovate".

That betrayal from a close aide, that last moment ditching from a client at a crucial time are things which will prepare you for extergencies and will automatically prepare you to change your work processes to account for such uncertainties.

The basic premise why some leaders are against B-schools is because there you are learnt to capture value from customers and less about creating value for your organisation.

Before B school grads start becoming sentimental, guys just hold your horses for a few moments and let me explain :

When we are taught marketing, you typically learn the importance of building and protecting your brand or doing quantitative analysis to identify customer segments and get customer feedback.

And the classic example of implementing the above is the "Tiger Gupta" edtech case, which claims to teach awesome coding to young kids and gives their parents an illusion of salaries in millions of dollars!!

Further, when there were litigations and claimants on their falsified claims, they did everything in their power to silence their sceptics - even their customers.

If one retrospects those, you will find a flaw in their thinking - which partly arose because of their learning!!

Let's now think from a learner's perspective and corroborate with an example - as always!!

Here we will consider an IIM - a prestigious institute in INDIA and amongst the top 100 B schools in the world.

So in the year 2008, a MBA from an IIM would cost around INR 500,000 and the salary one could get after 2 years of learning used to be INR 15,00,000. A good ROI.

Cut to 2021.

Today the IIM's charge upwards of INR 23,00,000 and offer a salary of around INR 25,00,000.

The same goes around for the Executive MBA programs too.

A 1 yr Executive MBA fees in 2009 in an IIM used to be: INR 20,00,000 and the salary then would be: INR 20,00,0000

Progressing to 2021, the same 1 yr Executive MBA fees has now come to INR 28,00,000 against a salary of INR 26,00,000.

This case research you can do for any MBA college and you would find the trend to be almost similar.

So what does this show?

This shows the diminishing value of the leading MBA in India over time.

The MBA is gasping for oxygen.

The books being used in MBA 15 years ago are still being used today.

The fees of the MBA program have grown several times but the content has not changed.

The MBA needs a makeover.

But what should the MBA program change into?

Dual specializations or specializations in newer areas like analytics & entrepreneurship.

Strangely the MBA programs in entrepreneurship do not teach any practical skills to start a business.

Specialized masters in analytics make you better skilled than an MBA in analytics

The MBA reminds me of the manager whose salary has grown but skills are the same. Eventually he gets laid off one day.

The MBA teaches you how to run a business.

With this money one can start a company & learn more about business than any MBA.

India needs more entrepreneurs today who will create jobs & employ the millions who are jobless.

We need a practical MBA program which should teach a person both how to build a business & run it.

So now as a reader - you should pause and think, If the MBA is any worth it?

So coming back to our premise of marketing - you will ask -

What should one do?

Well, for beginners you should initially ignore your brand (be it college you want to get into or company you are working for) and obtain all customer feedback through direct interaction, whether by experience, observation, or interviews.

As unconventional as it may sound, but rather than emphasizing on building brands by satisfying a broad range of customers through perfected products, one should emphasize on the need to test low-fidelity prototypes with small groups of customers, embracing errors as opportunities to learn and perfecting your product/service.

When you do that, it will become a constant learning curve and the opportunity of failure decreases.

Now you may think, marketing was an easy example. So let's dig deeper.

When we learn finance, we are typically taught about the marginal cost logic:

Where the importance of leveraging prior fixed-cost investments is with new initiatives.

This approach essentially tunes your brain to create an unknowing bias towards incremental innovation efforts.

As an entrepreneur or if you want to inculcate that kind of mindset, then you need to learn how to look for opportunities in building something disruptive, something that hasn't been built before, that solves a problem through a unique solution.

It is because we live in a world of uncertainty, where leveraging investments be a bad practice, as it may lead to building a workaround solution rather than one which nails the job to be done.

And before you judge me, let me again give the disclaimer - I am not discounting the role of B school managers in organizations or diminishing their value.

Both the approaches I gave above have their pros and cons. The key to success is to recognize when to apply the traditional B-school approach and when to apply entrepreneurial thinking. That's a decision the manager/entrepreneur has to take based on the level of uncertainty he is facing.

In other words, when you face a situation with uncertainty levels, it is wise to apply an entrepreneurial approach or mindset and when the uncertainty gets resolved, and you are back to the daily grind of your usual run-of-the-mill sort of problems, you should use the traditional B-school approach.

Chapter 2: Wading through a downturn

Three-quarters of companies experience a revenue decline during a recession, yet 14% actually experience revenue and profitability growth.

Some years ago, during an investor summit and I was at a party where I interacted with someone who was a board member at a large insurance company.

As drinks flowed and we got chatty about various topics and came the topic of a recession / stagflation or economic downturn as one may call.

Being the inquisitive self, I asked him his business was affected by the recession and how are things going?

The answer he gave is something, I will never forget and cleared my concepts of economy – which is common sense, but hardly any management book in colleges highlight it.

First, he gave a mocking look at me, for I should know the basics of his business!!

Undeterred by his look and after observing my blank expression, He said they were doing great.

In fact, as per him "Insurance always does fantastic when the economy is bad because when people get scared, they take out more insurance".

Now why am I mentioning about it here?

Because we should never forget that national crises which are bad for many people and cause much suffering for some are often fantastic for the ruling classes including business, media, politics and the wealthy.

That's why after 2-3 waves, most economies are open now despite the deaths, pain and hardship that 4th or future Covid waves will cause.

Same is happening in the Ukraine crisis as well.

Lives are being lost, people are being shifted, energy deficit has become a reality – but business is as usual with all parties, Europe is part of the war – yet business with Russia is usual (even more)!!

Business benefits because there are huge opportunities during hard times. Its why wealthy people love wars. Plus, they try and get plenty of tax benefits to milk from such instances!!

Want an example?

Look at all the pharma manufacturers of Covid vaccines and their soaring profits + the sops they availed to *"saving humanity"*.

The media benefits as people consume more news during crises, so they get link clicks and advertiser rates rise. Politicians benefit as they get to roar more without scrutiny when people are distracted, and because during anxious times people (usually) vote for incumbents.

Politicians also get to give huge grants and benefits to business which are then returned to them as campaign funding.

And NO, this isn't the idea of a particular country – but globally rampant practices.

Wealthy people benefit because the unbelievable tax practices get extended and consolidated, including government policies to ensure that ultimately real estate rises and tax write-offs for purchases happen. Plus, they own the businesses and media, of course to drive their agenda's.

These are dark days, folks.

But don't let them get you down.

Many a successful business have been started during a recession.

As ironical it may sound, I started my first business during a slow down and took advantage of few situations and business principles (which I will discuss) that helped me move ahead.

This will give you a different perspective than the traditional recession / depression doom & gloom.

I've come to the conclusion that no matter the state of the world economy, you still have to put in your efforts, what else are you going to do?

Can't just call it quits and start crying.

So what are we gonna do?

We need to follow the 4 Mantra's Of Going:

These are,

1. Being Present
2. Working With Available Stuff
3. Do What Sells
4. Keep Repeating

Miss any one of these, and you get a hard lesson from "reality".

1. Being Present

I believe in the famous quote of Eddie Kennison, "When opportunity presents itself, don't be afraid to go after it."

However, there is slight addition to it, he may have forgot to add.

Opportunity can present itself out of thin air – but it won't come searching for you with a placard on it's hand.

Opportunities don't find people.

They find a "time" and a "place".

And whoever is there at that "time" and "place", gets that opportunity. Thereon acting on that or not is a separate issue.

Simply "Being Present" puts you into the time and place where opportunities naturally come to you. In every venture, you will find that just because you have opened your shop – does not mean customers will come.

They will come – No doubt.

But when they do – You should be there to respond it!!!

There are many entrepreneurs, who never check emails or do so – once in a blue moon and if any opportunity may have arrived – you will have missed it.

The same stands true for any notifications on any business platform!!!

2. Working with Available Stuff

Being an engineer and a business person, I always believe in doing things myself. You can't shy from moping up the floor in the initial days.

If you do, you won't succeed.

Though I knew the mantra, once I deviated from this – because my co-founders forced and needless to say, we failed.

You need to first hone your strengths, work with all the available stuff you have to truly succeed.

All fancy things that your business needs – small or big, product or resource is available in the market.

But that comes at a cost.

When you divert your strengths or resources towards other things, your core starts to suffer.

So, let me explain with an example.

In one of my ventures, my co-founder came from a corporate world – where he was used to having a set of office staff for doing tasks!!

So when we started listing the pre-requisites, his list started with a few things like:
- Well furnished office
- Front Office staff
- Cleaning staff etc.

And I used to come from a different mindset, where I often started my hustle from my home and graduate to a co-working space.

The idea of well-furnished office, having secretarial staff, janitors etc in the initial days sounded fancy and cool and despite all the wisdom I throw in here, I had to agree.

Why?

Because, I wasn't the majority.

Needless to say, the initial few sales we did – did not even cover our "exorbitant" fixed costs and that ballooning costs never subsided.

Over the period of time, I had to excuse myself from the business – because there were a series of decisions like this taken, where despite having the knowledge or predicting the future, you can't do anything!!

However, this learning of being frugal stayed with me!

To make do, with whatever resources is the key!!

The same get's revalidated in kitchen as well.

You want to try some fancy dish and start preparing stuff and at some point you find, a few ingredients are missing from your shelf.

Here you have 3 recourses available.

First discard the idea of creating the dish and throwing away in trash whatever you have done.

Second, rushing to the nearby store to fetch the ingredients.

Third and the most vital part – Do your takeaways from the recipe and alter it accordingly.

You try to replace say a cashew-nut with peanut (that gives the rough texture) or totally skip that ingredient.

The vital aspect here is: Presenting a new dish.

A few changes here and there is your unique touch, but ultimate aim of serving a dish is fulfilled.

So rather than spending time on fancy crockery, fancy produce – let's first roll out the basic dish, then think later about making it fancy.

3. Do What Sells

One of the biggest blind spots is moving away from one's own perspective.

We are bombarded with information every day on what we should do and how we should do it – thanks to a ton of analytics apps and tracking software.

It takes a lot of discipline to look at "reality" the way it is, understand it and then use it to Do What Sells.

We are way too invested in our own opinions, ideologies and imagination without giving "reality" it's due respect.

Setting and achieving goals these days seem to be fueled by copying what others are doing.

We are always in an incognito mode of comparing with other.

Comparing our business (it's revenue/profits/share price/product mix/no. of employees/revenue per employee etc) with other's. Comparing with everyone else's system that works for them instead of identifying what works for us.

For one of my ventures, where we had VC money – we were always in a race.

First, comparing with the segment leader across all vanity metrics and just when you feel settled in with an aim, these investors jump in to rattle your ship.

They start comparing how their other portfolio companies are performing in some other metrics and how you are lagging behind.

At the end, we end up investing a lot of valuable time trying to match up to the expectations of others, so much so that, many of us have become frustrated with ourselves or even lost our way.

The pressure is real!

From youngsters getting heart diseases purely due to stress to some combating some real issues of depression.

Why not use the KISS (keep it simple silly) approach?

Let's just stick to what sells and not get into a race with others. Let just us be!!! Let's grow in our own pace and not indulge into other's pressure.

I often take TIME off from everyone, everything for introspection.

I spend time understanding myself/my organizations – to understand what I/we are, try to connect with inner true self, and then lead the path instead of the following without questioning.

I have had instances where I was doing things, taking business decisions (like product mix, marketing, branding, hiring etc) that didn't seem natural to me. It was being done to fit in, be in the trend or because it works best for your investors or whatever — it's not for you!

Your customer and your product, which sells should be the focus.

Let's take for instance an example of automobiles.

Before the era of Tesla, there were companies which had a vanity lineup of hybrid cars (based on the concept of hydrogen fuel cells etc) just for the sake of it.

But once competition caught up, they are no-where.

Because, those efforts were half-hearted and half-baked with products just for the sake of it.

The core mantra is:

Have a conviction, validate it and stick to it.

4. Keep Repeating

Heard about the power of compounding from your financial advisor while selling you an investment product?

Guess what, the same works for business albeit a different manner.

Imagine if you keep "Being Present" >> " Work With Available Stuff" >> "Do What Sells" and "Keep Repeating" everyday.

Building a business is akin to growing a tree. The power of compounding will make sure that you succeed even if you try not to. The wait is long and often frustrating. But if you stick to it, one day you'll get to harvest a bunch of delicious fruits.

At the end of it all,

Don't forget to take care of your mental health.

Don't panic and see the recession and be fearful of it.

See it as opportunity.

You need to self-affirm "Even in a recession, I thrive."

With a tough economy comes erratic consumer buying behavior, no doubt, but with the right tactics at your disposal - you can be rest assured that you'll stick it out unhurt.

God promised us in the midst of famine we'd have plenty.

We can't sit and wait for food to fall out the sky though.

Chapter 3: Renew, Rebrand or Refresh

C hange is the only truth and it's good;
      It always is, especially when it concerns brands that have to remain relevant despite continuously evolving market dynamics and consumer sensibilities.

Let's start this chapter with a "live" example from history!!

There were 2 companies : A & B which were present in the food business, particularly cereal segement.

During the Great Depression, Company A significantly reduced it's advertising budget and rival company B took advantage of it and doubled marketing spend, investing heavily advertising and introduced new products.

Guess what happened?

Well, B's profits grew by 30% and the company became the market leader, a position it has maintained for decades.

Here B is Kellogg's, while A is Post Consumer Brands.

In a hard economy (like the one we are witnessing), one of the smartest things to do is to always roll-out NEW products or remodel your products to fit in.

I'll give you another example...

If you visit India, Maruti Suzuki is the No.1 car manufacturer and has a huge market share.

During the chip crisis of 2022, all car manufacturers had cut back on their advertising spends – because they were unable to deliver products and their output had reached threshold.

Now, while industry was offering new age features like connected car tech, or hybrid or more fuel-efficient diesel engines – you would expect the likes of Maruti to cherish their brand loyalty and leadership.

But they came out aggressively with marketing.

Let me remind you, they did not have those fancy connected car features or EV or even a diesel engine.

So, what did they market?

Their existing gasoline engines, which have been there for sometime and same old features.

Crazy, right?

But how did they sell?

Well, they repackaged products.

Maruti took a leaf out of Volkswagen's playbook, which is keep adding/deleting features from your existing line-up and keep giving slight makeovers/ limited edition names to your products.

In this way, without spending much on new platforms or line-ups – Maruti kept pushing the old products in a slightly new avatar and was able to maintain it's dominant position – by tickling of serving to its customers sentiments of having something new.

Another thing that is vital and complementary in nature to repackaging is repositioning.

Blackberry smart phones became a rage all over the world, only because they repositioned. They went from being a business phone for professionals to being a device for people to stay connected with each other.

But now the Blackberry game is over as it failed to adapt and Apple's I-phone is back with a bang as the "new in thing".

Competitive advantage can be attained through creative packaging and campaigns (sometimes witty) so that a consumer selects your product just by looking at it, he may not even have heard about the product before, but the packaging is assertive enough to showcase you as a trustworthy product enough for him to purchase it.

Companies need to adapt quickly to the changing needs of the market, it's the only way to attract new customers and retain existing ones. So, cutting down on your marketing budget always does more harm than good.

The mantra is simple, adapt or make way for the competitor

Now launching a product is easy, but re-launching is Risky without infuriating customers!!!

This is more so with digital products or apps.

In the spirit of staying trendy, you change the UI/UX or add newer features but it enrages customers, because sometimes it brings in a hindrance to normal usage.

Customers are baffled by the 'newness' and their inability to use their products, which leads to a bigger problem of customer attrition.

In the end, it always costs more to fix a problem in order to save the brand once something's gone wrong.

Remember, it's faster and cheaper to go slow, invest more upfront, and obtain a clear understanding of the consumer to lay the proper foundation. Only then will your best intentions go right.

I learnt a lot from the 2008 recession (or you may call it depression).

One of it is not to listen to everyone because you'll hear so many negatives and fear will creep in.

The oxygen you need right now is sales and more sales. The only way to get those sales without much resistance and skepticism is by marketing more.

And the only way to market more is to keep tinkering with your product, product-mix once in a while, re-packaging the products to give it a new feel.

Even with books –

Customers love the smell of a new book; the touch of raw paper and you find re-prints and editions after editions for 100-year-old book in the shelf of Crossword selling today.

Where does the old one sell?

Probably at some dinky shop for a few dollars.

The collector's edition is an exception and limited to only a few. If we are in the growth game, we need to roll-out new products – this in carnal rule cannot be avoided.

For the clients I consult, I always them that marketing is to a business what oxygen is to humans.

I read an interesting interview of Sam Walton, the founder of Wal-Mart where he was asked about his views on recession?

He responded, "I thought about it and decided not to participate."

You can either get yourself or your team together to find a way out or you can just scream like others and you'll sink (God forbid!)

Chapter 4: The Art of Dropping It

Now we read about entrepreneurship, the kind of mindset it requires, the kind of people we need to hire, growing in times of crisis and how to keep the spirit of 'newness' alive.

All said and done, there needs to be a point where you need to let it go.

There have been examples like Ola Used Cars – which started and closed a business within a matter of 8 months or food delivery startups that close down within a period of few months of inception.

So when should you hold it?

When should you drop it?

What should you drop?

These are some vital questions, each entrepreneur goes through.

"Pivot" – has created more confusion than solving problems. Too much pivot and you are dead – because it consumes up essential resources and time.

If you don't pivot, there is no innovation and probably competition has already killed you.

So here we will discuss on two main aspects:

- When to kill an idea
And
- When to kill a strategy

Incidentally, both are linked to each other – yet there is an ocean of difference amongst them.

So let's begin:

When to kill an idea

Every successful business begins its life as an idea.

Now before you jump your horses, let me also add – more than 99% enthusiasts never act on their ideas, it always stays on paper!!!

To give you context,

I have this relative who happens to be in a senior position in a bank.

Whenever (I mean actually every time) we would go to his house, our pass-time would be to discuss business ideas after dinner.

His partner-in-crime would be my dad, who also happens to be a banker!!

So both, bankers by profession would sit across dinner table – discuss the various projects they have financed. Now, they may have gone through innumerous business proposals, projections in their life and have sanctioned many of them too. So, their discussion would be serious – with all details about making it successful and which business venture one would do.

After hours of discussion, when it is close to midnight and both seniors have reached their epitome of being awake, they conclude on a particular idea and how they would execute it. With this they would be bid adieu for a night and sleep (literally sleep) over the idea and next morning it's a clean slate.

Next time (which happens to be after few months) when they meet, the story would repeat.

Thing is, they may have been successful professionals – but that got them attached, to certainty, to being risk averse and they lack the courage to venture into the unknown, to face uncertainty and jump to make this work!!!

And this is not something limited to them.

More than 90% people I have met, may have big business ideas, but ask them to leave their job, jump and execute their idea – if it is so foolproof and believe me 99% of the lot would back out!!

Dunno if they don't have conviction on their own ability or their own idea.

I per se, have learnt it the hard-way for trusting on such kind of people – because they will never truly commit to the cause and just piggyback on your success.

Never take business idea from a person who fears uncertainty or does not have the courage to troubleshoot real world problems!!

Most people ask me, do I follow my gut regarding a business logic/idea or how do I know if an idea will succeed?

Well, it's part gut and partly killing an idea.

With your gut feeling and experience you have to kill your own idea i.e. search for its weaknesses, uncover its vulnerabilities, and seek to discover all the reasons why it won't work.

Risk is always a part of a new venture.

But when you try to kill your own idea, you will demarcate key metrics – where you need to detach yourself emotionally and take the hard decision of pivoting or shutting it out. This helps cover the decision bias that is part of being us as a human being.

And while doing this, you sub-consciously calibrate yourself to be fully aware of the tactical and execution risks that you must overcome.

You may ask if there is a blueprint to killing an idea?

Well, there indeed is one – Three rules that works for me at least:

i) Listen to people around you:

Being drunk in the spirit of entrepreneurship and being drunk in alcohol exhibit the same symptoms.

You may have often seen, the person who is drunk feels he is always right, emotional about his feelings and is over-confident.

Two pegs down and in India, my friends can fly a jumbo-jet with the confidence that they get!!!

That's how entrepreneurs think – their business will fly to moon and they will only make profits!!!

As a rule, never drink with people who ain't your well-wishers, as they may take advantage of your situation.

Similarly, don't discuss your ideas with only YES Men, or those who have vendetta's (like investing cheap on you, getting hired themselves, selling their product, or want you to fail etc). Surround yourself with different kind of people – your true well-wishers, your nemesis, yes men and all other variety you can find.

Discuss your idea with them!!

Even with the elevator operator, while taking the ride with him.

Everyone has a different perspective and listen to everyone's thoughts – more so, of the random stranger and your well-wisher.

If you are not able to satiate their curiosity with your answers, you should probably be aiming for the dust-bin with your idea – how great it may be!!!

ii) Be Pessimistic all the time

Now, how can be an entrepreneur (who is supposed to be optimistic) be pessimistic all the time?

Am I suggesting you to develop split-personality disorder?
Probably, NOT!!

You will agree to the fact that human mind keeps wandering from one goal post to another!

In a typical week, my wife keeps asking me to plan for next vacation (even if I my last vacation's EMI is still not finished) or about buying house or next asset for her, atleast 4-5 times.

If I were to exhibit optimism to her queries, my whole financial planning would be in shambles.

As an entrepreneur, you have set your priorities and chalked out a finance plan – what to indulge, when to indulge and what to avoid.

Same happens in our business life too;

I may be a creative person, my company maybe promoting innovation; But in our day-to-day ops, my tendency and that of every manager should be to kill new ideas that can get us off track or make us go over budget.

It's all about timing – scheduled time when you are open to hitting the board with random cool ideas to brainstorm and solve problems, where you let new ideas take wings – but not all the time!

iii) Be Greedy with your resources

Running a successful business does not mean, you or your team can spendthrift.

Everyday I am inundated with a few dozen messages selling me some cool analytic or customer care or some other feature enhancing product over email or through Linkedin.

Can I entertain every one of them?

Some products may inspire you with a new idea that seems compelling and would be a great addition to your product suite.

But will it really make an impact to the end purpose?

We need to introspect,

What is the problem we're trying to solve?

Who are the people we're trying to serve?

If you stay focused on the end result, it's easier to kill the tantalizing vanity distractions along the way.

Every month there is a sob story on the internet, how tech teams while adding vanity add-ons forget about their cloud capabilities and founders are left astonished when they receive a huge bill from their cloud hosting provider.

What they did is, let their guard off for building the awesome product – and now they don't have cash for the product to sustain!!!

Prioritize, start with a NO and gradually work to YES for an expenditure and perhaps you can wade through successfully.

Now to the next part:

When to kill a strategy

Most businesses have failed because of reliance on wrong consultants.

These days the fancy consulting companies only care about their bottom-line and less about their customers. These strategy consultants come in, show their exuberance while data collection in your office, document a new strategy in a shiny well formatted presentation with a weighty report.

Then town hall meetings get organized, where employees are told to change their behavior, scorecards are reformulated and balanced, budgets set aside to support new initiatives.

And then nothing happens.

At Grazing Minds, we have encountered customers who were earlier served by these fancy firms – who have a global brand name, driven by highly paid grads from top colleges – adept in making assumptions, but lack real world experience and hardly done anything themselves. They are the MBA lot, we discussed in chapter 1 which successful entrepreneurs want to stay away from!!!

Now, why does such typical consulting report driven strategies don't yield any results?

It is often because they are not strategies at all.

Any real world strategy should involve a clear set of choices that define what the firm/client should and should NOT do.

Many strategies fail to get implemented, despite the best of people, because they do not represent a set of clear choices.

Let's give an example:

"We want to be the number one or number X, in Y market where which we operate" is a standard goal, which many consultants confuse to a strategy!!

The above statement does not tell you what you are going to do; all it does is tell you what you hope the outcome will be.

But you'll still need a strategy to achieve it.

Some go a step more refined, say:

"We want to increase operational efficiency; we will target Asia and Africa; and we will divest business X".

These may be excellent road-maps, but they together do not form a strategy. If you are made to jump into an implementation process without a clear strategic direction, you are doomed to fail.

Here also, I rely on three frameworks that work - for me at least:

i) Communicate your logic

You need to have a clear business logic which should be easy to communicate. This needs to be understood by each and every employee.

You cannot be having a list of 10-20 choices, as your employees will simply not remember them. And if they don't remember them, the choices cannot influence their behavior, in which case you have no strategy (but merely a PowerPoint deck).

Only communicating alone is not enough. Your employees need to understand the reasoning behind your business logic, believe them and follow them up in their day-to-day work.

ii) Not just a top-down process

A major reason, why many implementation efforts fail is that executives see it as a pure top-down, two-step process: "The strategy is made; now we implement it."

That's unlikely to work.

A successful strategy execution process is seldom a one-way trickle-down cascade of decisions.

No doubt, you indeed need a clear, top-down strategic direction.

But this will only be effective if, at the same time, you enable your employees to create bottom-up initiatives that fall within the boundaries set by that strategic intent.

iii) Organic selection

A common mistake in the bottom-up implementation process is that many top managers cannot resist doing the selection themselves.

They look at the various initiatives that employees propose as part of the strategy execution process and then they pick the ones they like best.

In contrast, top executives should resist the temptation to decide what projects live and die within their firms.

You need to give your managers ample autonomy to decide which project they wanted to work on, so projects that few people believed in automatically failed to get staffed.

Be brave enough to resist making these bottom-up choices, but design a system that does it for you.

iv) Let "change" be your default mode

Another reason many implementation efforts fail is that they usually require changing people's habits and it's easier said than done. Habits can't be changed by telling people in meeting or through circular, that they should act differently.

People are often not even aware that they are doing things in a particular way and that there might be different ways to run the same process.

Identifying and countering the bad habits that keep your strategy from getting executed is a daunting task in itself and there are various practices you can build into your organization to make it work.

It may involve reshuffling people into different departments, to disrupt and alter their habitual way of working and to expose people to alternative way of doing things.

There are usually different ways of doing things, and there is seldom one perfect solution, since all alternatives have advantages and disadvantages — whether it concerns an organization's structure, incentive system, or resource allocation process.

Hence change should be our default mode, to learn and grow.

And there are people who fear change,

Well time to change – when you let go off ideas, processes, people and thoughts that bind you to the unseen shackles of comfort, this leads to growth!!!

Chapter 5: Vanquishing the Social Devil

When I hear the word social media, the first thing that crosses my mind is connecting with people.

Social media (SM) has become a non- separable part of our lives. But, for many of us, it has become a mere game about the number of likes and comments we get on our posts or how recognized we are in the world of social media.

Call it fortunate or unfortunate – reaching the Gen X, Y, Z has become easier and difficult – both at the same time.

Easier because advertisers, influencers and social media platforms will show you ways to strengthen your audience, increase your reach with fancy packages.

Difficult, because the easier part was you buying a package in a world full of bots and leads that don't convert.

Difficult part is reaching your target audience, maintaining relationship with them, nurturing it to an extent to convert to sales. It becomes even more difficult when you have to abide by the platform's innumerous rules and yet you are at the mercy of their whims and fancies.

For those running million-dollar corporations, these social media platforms will bend backwards to accommodate your stance, help you get rid of negativity (bad press, negative reviews, employee rant or any kind of negative aspects) around your brand. But till the time you reach the million-dollar level, you will be hounded.

There have been numerous cases, where home-grown brand and small entrepreneurs after having invested a sizeable amount of time and money, find their accounts banned for some lame reason or the other.

So what happens then?

Your so-called *organic reach* gets a big blow.

So, the focus of small brands should be to bring audience and potential customers to channels of communication you own – like mailing lists, your blog etc.

In this way, if the social media companies or even your rival brands play mischief – you have access to your *"followers"* and re-engage with them without having to spend big.

SM has gained so much power that, the most successful businesses (particularly D2C), political parties, films would not have been this much fortunate if social media had not been there. It does change the pace, scale, and cost of communication. You can send more messages to more people, more quickly and more cheaply, than ever in history. But what you are going to say does not change just because you are using more efficient technology.

In my initial days of business, I was floated with the idea that you must have a certain number of followers to be taken seriously – which I can now say is false.

Because it takes so much work to get real Social Media followers, shortcuts can be tempting so you/your team resorts to buying fake followers/bots.

In my opinion, you don't need fakes, but only need the right audience.

So for Grazing Minds I paid zilch for social media marketing. I wasn't impressed by vanity metrics of followers or likes!!

I believed in the power of organic and understood my audience was different.

So tell you with numbers,

We catered to CXO's for consulting and professionals for finance learning programs and relied heavily on LinkedIn for creating our organic audience.

Now, if I were to expect the same number of followers across LinkedIn, TikTok, Insta, Twitter, FB, Pinterest or Youtube – that would be absurd.

We had segmented our customer base and we understood that our target audience on LinkedIn was hardly present or interacted on other platforms. As a result – today we have $1/3^{rd}$ the number of audiences across other platforms, as we do on LI and we are okay with it.

When you define your target audience, it means you understand that not EVERYONE IS FOR YOU.

Remember though, the only way to get your target audience is to post the right content. Because no matter how many sponsored ads you put up, NOTHING CAN MAKE UP FOR BAD CONTENT.

Recently there was a fad amongst creative agencies to forcefully hurt sentiments of people at large or creating controversies by creating ads that were distasteful to many.

As a result, this led to virality of the campaign, the brand, the product and all the company had to do was – make an apology and recall the ad.

Now, there has to be something ethical in marketing which needs to be followed.

And I ain't referring to any particular country or a particular product segment.

This strategy of stoking a controversy with distasteful ads or indulging controversial people surely does grab eye balls but does more harm to your brand in long-run than ever.

Today's customers may have a short memory, but that is true for product features. Rub them the wrong side on sentiments and the effects may last for a good period of time.

So the crux is, the community you engage with – you should add value to it, rather than dividing the community as a whole. You don't need regulator or some censor body to tell that to you , rather your internal mechanism should echo such kind of sentiment.

Offer Value to your customers using social media.

Example- If you are into selling clothes

Don't only advertise your products but

Give dressing advice to clients, etc.

That'll ensure that they're invested in your businesses social media pages and it low-key gives a better chance of your product being advertised side by side.

As a business owner, you just need to understand how to leverage social media properly, if you really want to grow.

So how do you do that?

At Grazing Minds and DH Holdings we have established a few fundamental laws which we adhere to. Here is a list of the same for you to take inspiration:

i) Listen thy customer:

Success with social media and content marketing requires more listening and less talking. Read your target audience's online content and join discussions to learn what's important to them. Only then can you create content and spark conversations.

ii) The benefit of being focused:

It's better to specialize than to be a jack-of-all-trades. A highly-focused social media and content marketing strategy intended to build a strong brand has a better chance for success than a broad strategy that attempts to be all things to all people.

iii) Quality trumps all:

For social media, it's quality always trumps quantity, but many never follow it. It's better to have 1,000 online connections who read, share and talk about your content with their own audiences than 10,000 connections who disappear after connecting with you the first time.

iv) Use influence where needed:

It's wise to spend time with online influencers in your market niche, who have quality audiences and are likely to be interested in your products, services and business. Connect with these leaders and work to build relationships with them.

v) Patience is the key:

What many marketeers tend to misunderstand is that social media and content marketing success doesn't happen overnight. It's a long term process.

While it's possible to catch lightning in a bottle, it's far more likely that you will need to commit to the long haul to achieve results with Social Media.

vi) Power of Compounding:

As we have discussed earlier, doing something daily evokes the power of compounding – vital for growth. If you consistently publish good quality content & work to building your audience of quality followers, who engage with you – your social strength increases. This sharing of content opens new entry points for search engines like Google to find it in keyword searches.

vii) Distributing Value:

In the initial days of my social media marketing, I used to spend all time on social media directly promoting our products and services. Not to mention, we did not get as much traction as required.

You will not promote someone else's products, unless of-course it's another clickbait for some kind of referral contest.

Well today, the customer has grown up and such clickbaits don't work.

You must add value to the conversation. Focus less on conversions and more on creating amazing content and developing relationships.

Once the customer looks up to your posts, relates with your brand – conversions will follow.

viii) Acknowledge Everyone:

Think of your social media assets as your offline assets. If someone reaches your office, you couldn't and wouldn't ignore them – so there is no point ignoring someone just because the relationship is online.

Infacts, brands these days are even engaging with trolls and smartly shutting them out.

Building relationship is key of social media marketing success, so always acknowledge every person who reaches out to you. This creates the bond and not to forget, others are looking how you are engaging with people,

Opportunity to earn some brownie points there!!!

So if you are an entrepreneur, freelancer, or if your job is heavily linked to being on social media – the above rules if followed will definitely bring about a remarkable impact on your social media strategy!

Chapter 6: Don't Indulge Even If On Fire

Any company that adds a "tech" to its industry like fintech, edtech, proptech, regtech etc have historically led the way in showering employees with perks, ranging from free meals and generous vacation packages to on-site gyms and movie theaters. And now other industries are following suit. In fact, some brazen founders are offering BMW bikes or Macs as joining bonus and to ensure that employees join on the fixed date.

Such is the competition and pressure for retaining employees during a boom period. Add to it, the changing technological dynamics mean – you are constantly bombarded with a variety of interesting tech to be incorporated in your business/product which may or may not add value to your business but surely does add vanity.

Now, how much of this vanity affairs should you indulge in?

Sometimes business guru's say that extravagance is necessary in business, to succeed.

Their logic was that, customers should look upto the brand and its owners as epitome of over-indulgence and by using their product, they get to experience a part of that indulgence or extravagance. It is because of this logic that you will find that the likes of Richard Branson, Tony Fernandes and even Vijay Mallya led a life of much large picture, which many couldn't attain.

Now some could say that their industry needed opulence.

But things have changed!!!

Recently a picture emerged in social media and even newspapers about Rahul Bhatia (even you can google it out)!!

Now for starters, Rahul Bhatia is the billionaire promoter and MD of Interglobe Enterprises, which runs IndiGo airlines also. Now IndiGo is the largest airline in India with over 53% market share and amongst the prominent low-cost airline in S.E. Asia.

Coming back to the picture, why it's in news!!

So as I said earlier, some people think that the airline biz is full of fashion, opulence, extravagance and indulgence.

Well, that was the "presumed norm" earlier and those who followed it have failed terribly. In fact, the fall had been so terrible that many employees, investors and to an extent customers also have lost a decent sum.

In this era of failures, rises the story of IndiGo.

As a product, it never offered any premium-ness or never indulged its customers to feel extravagance. All it did was, provide on-time and hygienic service while making you move from one place to another.

No fuss no muss.

In the recent news report, the founder of IndiGo was travelling in his own airline – in an economy class seat (as IndiGo is an all economy carrier), enjoying a cup of tea (served during their on-board service) with a packet of everyday glucose biscuit costing INR 10 (0.13 USD)!!

Passengers who were on-board the same flight, hardly knew they were travelling with the boss of the airline.

The context is, Mr.Bhatia with all the assets and net-worth at his disposal, chose to be frugal in his journey. Now this maybe, because he was gauging customer sentiment as a normal passenger or he was truly frugal in his lifestyle.

But you get the context!

When you are frugal in your choices, your employees get the message that you mean business. There is no wastage and over-indulgence is a big NO!!

As a result, the enterprise works towards profitability and Indi-Go is a big case study in this sector, the only airline that has managed to be profitable and has a bank balance so huge – others can only envy.

So, you gotta learn from the leader - The way to wealth is as plain as the way to market.

Now being frugal doesn't mean slashing your spending or depriving yourself of things that you enjoy. It simply means understanding the true value of a penny that you are going to spend and thereby making every conscious effort to get the maximum returns from it.

As easy as it may sound, during my consulting gigs with small business owners – the most common trait all of them had is their struggle evaluating the difference between smart financial decisions and blanket cost-cutting.

There is a fine line which they never seem to find!

Companies cannot grow by cutting costs but by increasing sales. (And this very basic fundamental is what differentiates a business owner from an employee mindset).

An employee if asked to lower expenses will in the zest to perform deprive essential business systems of needed capital, which leads to stagnant growth or negative cash flow.

A true entrepreneur understands the unintended consequences of not spending money on important business systems.

Some business owners think they are frugal, while in reality they are being cheap, which shows in the end product or even during internal processes.

Remember, frugality leads to efficiency while being cheap leads to a whole host of new problems.

Being frugal in business means you look past the short-term solution and consider the big-picture consequences with respect to time and money and its impact on your brand and sales.

And it's nothing new to be introduced, rather over ancestors have been using it – just that they never sold the concept clearly!!!

Benjamin Franklin, the founding father of the United States was famous for his judicious usage of resources.

Ever heard of the quotes like "Haste makes waste", or "Rather go to bed without dinner than to rise in debt", well – these were some of his famous works!!

Some cultures have naturally followed frugal innovation due to limited resources and lack of finance. The Great Indian Jugaad Innovation is one such concept. Jugaad is a Hindi word that means an improvised solution born from ingenuity and cleverness, to make do and find ways to do things because of the lack of resources.

The crux of it is that constant innovation is challenging and requires continued resilience.

Ben Franklin, who was a self-made man - understood the dangers of living as if one has means, when in fact they do not. And Covid, taught us the ramifications!!

With paycuts etc, so many people dwindled up on high interest loans that it got difficult for them to survive, Infact, Covid also taught us how to lead life with minimalism.

Dunno about others, but I understood how much I could save by not stepping out, not over-indulging on stuff which could totally be avoided!!!

The same holds true for business too.

Frugality in business does not mean that you don't spend or to raise money.

It's about spending money on what you know is going to bring you clear value, and raising money when you have clear need to do so.

Frugal entrepreneurship and frugal innovation, in simple terms is a mindset and approach to creating new products or services that focus on sustainable growth and inclusivity at scale. It's a lean approach to innovation that is essentially faster, better, cheaper, and more sustainable.

There have been umpteen examples, when founders have raised humongous amounts of money like crazy and going bust in about 6 months time!

I mean, it's fine if you have a runway of 6 months, but when your last round was at a splendid valuation – you need to be judicious about spending resources.

Another much-discussed phenomenon in the startup world in recent years, is celebrating fund-raise!!

Raising money for your venture is, and should always be, treated as a means to an end. It is not necessarily a business accomplishment and without the right game plan it may very well be the reason for your failure!

Actually, having too much money in your business launch is wasteful. It can lead to lazy and inefficient business decisions.

Starting a company does not need to cost a lot of cash.

After a series of failed tech IPOs in the recent past, many are finding it difficult in raising money. And there comes the "Do or Die" moment for startups to raise money in order to stay afloat.

Now some of these startups could have mitigated the crisis, if they'd been observing the art of frugality in their business venture all along.

Large, airy open-floor workspaces in the most coveted business district.

Huge joining bonuses.

Paid PR with interviews and pictures on magazines and blogs or even that paid *"X under X award"*.

Break room with all the games and fixtures, some even having fancy beers or kombuchas – on demand.

These are all expenditures one typically associates with successful startup that has established itself, or is looking to do so.

Here's the thing: **You don't need this to be successful.**

In most cases, you don't even need a dedicated office space, as many companies discovered during Covid lockdowns.

The hustle culture and hyper-growth forced down by VC's to their portfolio companies, follow the mantra of: Raise, Scale and Exit.

Now, this path is not for everyone.

Even many unicorns are now finding this the hard way, in the current climate – where they are forced to close, months after gaining the unicorn status.

Therein lays a middle path, which has methodical growth and careful scaling for your startup.

I have followed a ***"D.I.P.S"*** method, whenever I venture into a new business and hope that helps you all too!

1. Making Smart **Decisions**:

The most crucial aspect for your enterprise is to gain customers, for which people need to know about its existence.

If you have bag loads of cash, there are numerous marketing agencies and performance marketing companies that can help you out. But they come at a huge cost, as outsourcing any advertising or marketing task is highly expensive.

And as a new or small business owner, you necessarily don't even have to spend a ton of money on a PR firm. Today, the market is flush with various user-friendly, inexpensive marketing tools like, you can create social media accounts and promote your business for free using social media marketing.

You can also hold flash events and sales.

Events draw in more people, which increases sales and encourages repeat customers. As you market your startup, remember to keep the conversation going about your brand and stay visible to your target customers.

1. Keep another **Income**:

One advice I often give to grads coming out of college, it's fine if you have learnt about entrepreneurship -but don't jump into the ship as a fresher!

Often, entrepreneurs are natural-born risk takers.

But you need capital to start it and you could get into serious debt if you're not as successful as you anticipated and that becomes more disastrous if you start on borrowed capital – from friends, family or worse a mortgaged loan.

You need to have another source of ***Income***, which helps you to fall back on if your idea isn't profitable.

Before I was a business owner, I worked part-time gigs giving presentations, doing consultations for businesses. Although I was going places, being an entrepreneur was in my DNA.

You will know when you're ready to go all in on your startup.

1. **Plan** Ahead:

Let me be honest, that when I began my company, I did not plan every detail. At odd 23 years, I felt like my entrepreneurial clock was ticking, and I was running out of time. Jumping into entrepreneurship was exhilarating, but I ended up making some decisions that cost me dearly.

Growing a business takes preparation.

Working out ideas and researching some frugal business tips from business veterans before you launch a startup will save you time and money.

To map out your startup, it is essential draft a business plan - that should include everything from your mission to financial projections. It should be a blueprint of what you want to accomplish and how to accomplish it.

Evaluate all your costs and your sources of income. How much you can afford to launch your company and for how many days?

Make sure you're mentally, emotionally and financially prepared to start a business before taking the entrepreneurial leap.

Of course, one can't plan for everything in business. Whether something works for or against you, unexpected events do come up.

While you can't prepare for everything, you can take steps to help you navigate obstacles.

Your business plan will change as your company grows. You will have new needs and face different challenges, so revise your plan often.

Remember one thing: Almost all business problems will have solutions.

Some expensive, Some Reasonable and Some Affordable.

The one's that your consultants give you will be the most expensive – as covering their charges will be one of the major overheads.

The most affordable one will be the one, you find from your own research.

However the most reasonable one will be, from someone who has wide industry knowledge and gives you solution that resembles or backs with extensive research, is affordable and charges you accordingly so as to not dent your finances.

1. **Space** Well:

When it comes to your products and services, you have to provide top-notch quality, without a doubt. However, when you start your workspace could be a different story. You might have to sacrifice personal luxuries to work on growing your business.

As I stated earlier, don't be tempted to rent a fancy office or hire staff if it's not in your budget. A spick span office does not translate into a successful company.

In the initial days of your business, it's wise to put your money towards growing your brand rather than satiating your ego.

You can add extra perks once you're making decent profits.

Almost all my businesses started out of my study and with my personal computer – without any fancy stuff. But we were able to deliver, grow our business, and eventually move into a coveted corporate office.

Always remember, your first workspace is almost always temporary. As your business grows, so does your office. When you're starting out, focus on the moves that will help your company rise.

Even today, I am so comfortable with my home office that during Covid lockdowns – I felt like in the zone of growth and my productivity touched the roof, reminding me of old days.

It also gives me a sense of confidence and relief, both at the same time.

Confidence that, all I need to start a new business is a rock-solid idea and belief in self.

My initial seed requirements are low as compared to others because I can start frugally to be viable in the minimal of resources and so my chances of failure also decreases marginally,

Or in other words, because I am able to implement frugal practices and believe in not splurging over extravagance, I have a higher chance of achieving success.

And in such cut-throat competition, that slight high chance of success is enough to bolster my confidence and spirit to take that leap of faith into the unknown and start that new venture!

Chapter 7: Analytics Genie To The Rescue

With every slowdown, 99% enterprises make the same old mistakes of : resizing down, letting people go, shrinking, and hoping to tide over the crisis. However, growth-oriented organizations capitalize on this as a business opportunity – an opportunity to leverage their data that enables them to "do more with less".

Oil or not, data is an asset most companies already have. You don't have to go about exploring it in the blind. However, for most the problem lies in understanding what to do with their wealth of data.

Data can help an enterprise ward off the impact of a slowdown by providing insights for better targeting the market, instances to save money, and opportunities to increase profits.

The companies that respond best to slowdown are the ones that are most prepared for it.

And as compared to earlier slowdown, the positive part of this time's slowdown is the various plug and play technologies that are readily available to just sit on your processes (however legacy it maybe) and harness the gold mine of data, you never knew existed.

Top consultants believe that slowing sales during a slowdown is a good time to shift focus on technology and look at that part of a business. While some believe, it's better to not wait until you are hit by a slow-down to begin your digital transformation journey.

Slow-down or not, embracing new age digital tools is a must for sustenance.

If one acts before the slowdown, it allows a company to be proactive, rather than reactive, with its data. And since it could take time to put the necessary tools in place, depending on where your organization is with its technology, it's better to already have the tools to navigate the recession rather than wait until after the dust settles to start from scratch.

Growth-oriented enterprises, that are able to harness this data on-time employ the concept of Nanoeconomics to drive Precision Decisions to retain their customers, force their competitors' most important customers to migrate with better offerings, corner market share, create new revenue opportunities, and optimize or even re-invent key business and operational processes, procedures, and policies.

It is because of this reason, there has been a demand in the courses of Data Science in college level and those fellas with a Data Science degree are in high demand!!

Infact, such is the rage that every firm is looking for Data Scientists and 3rd party HR agencies are tired of looking for Data scientists looking to migrate, wooing them with offers on behalf of their clients and yet, these candidates ditching at the last moment.

It was actually the great recession of 2008 that catapulted the usage of analytics into mainstream enterprises as a way to save money on operations and achieve efficiency.

During slowdown, when every penny counts - leaders at companies big or small need to be judicious in their spending resources. Making tradeoffs is extremely difficult and it's here that product analytics becomes indispensable with its tight, impactful analytics and insights that help optimize programming, spots opportunities and spurs innovation. It shows companies what is and isn't working with their products, what to prioritize, and what to invest in.

At Grazing Minds, we've created a product-analytics dashboard to spot and help us remedy issues that could arise from a slowdown, as well as identify opportunities to go on the offensive and increase market share.

When I shared the dashboard during our company openhouse, my team suggested we open it up to everyone so that others can benefit from it ♥.

If this framework resonates and you want to learn how you can replicate it, please drop me a note.

I'm genuinely excited to help share how we're approaching the current macroeconomic uncertainty and provide some practical steps you can use to best prepare and navigate through it.

Here what we are essentially trying to track are a handful of early-warning signals or metrics that will alert us of a impending slowdown that has the capability to negatively affect our business. For instance, a slowing enrollment rate MoM basis can alert us of a negative economic effect near the horizon – giving us enough headroom to re-design our curriculum and courses to better align our learners, so that they are not affected by job-cuts due to renewed skills.

However, the impacts vary from company to company – depending on size and region. For example, we could see demand from startups decline before more mature businesses. We could see a geographic divergence based on many factors leading up to today and local response after the downturn. But again, anything can happen, which is why it is essential to track various metrics that give us a comprehensive view of our business. Here are some of the metrics I believe in constantly having a tab on:

> **Tech ecosystem metrics**

Tech layoffs from the Layoffs.fyi tool – Layoffs are a key indicator of economic health. Tracking layoffs in the tech sector from Layoffs.fyi gives us insight into whether companies in our sector have healthy balance sheets and available resources.

Funding rounds closed from Crunchbase – Funding rounds are a key indicator of economic health and appetite for risk in the tech sector. During previous downturns, the number of funding rounds decreased, so tracking funding rounds is a good way to judge market conditions.

> **Demand metrics**

Web traffic – The number of people visiting our website or app is a good top-level indicator of awareness of Grazing Minds.

Signups and people who've asked to be contacted by sales – Further down the funnel, the volume of people who have signed up for Grazing Minds and requested sales contact them shows how well we are attracting new users and businesses.

Growth plan purchases – Our Growth Plan is one of our most popular introductory plans. Tracking the number of purchases made gives us a baseline for the level of demand for our product.

New business forecasts – Including forecasts for new business helps guide our expectations.

> **Customer adoption and retention metrics**

Percentage of paid customers and percentage of Annual Recurring Revenue with healthy adoption – We have a threshold for how many weekly active users an account should have for us to consider them very unlikely to churn. We are tracking the percentage of our paid customers and percentage of Annual Recurring Revenue that meets or exceeds this threshold.

Churn and upsell forecasts – We input our forecasts for churn rate and potential upsells to track our customers' retention and expansion rates.

Quirky and varied Insights can help enterprises to predict which parts of their solutions or services are most likely to prosper or fail under which economic circumstances.

Based on the data about which solutions and products are performing optimal in the market, companies can extend data mining to discover cross-selling and up-selling opportunities to ramp up revenues.

In today's era there is practically a plethora of datasets available which can help minimize losses in an economic slowdown.

The bottom line is that the application of Business Analytics software and tools should not be deemed extravagant during economic slowdowns. Instead, it should be seen as a vital technology tool that should be leveraged across all business actions – from discovering revenue opportunities, preventing frauds, getting rid of fund wastage, optimizing the workforce, and even sales and marketing.

Chapter 8: When Mythology Inspires

Nah, don't worry – this ain't gonna be spiritual or move in any direction away from entrepreneurship learning.

I believe in a simple logic –

"History teaches if we are willing to learn".

Now this learning can come from the stories we hear from our parents/grand-parents, from history books and if we go a bit farther – from the fables.

I believe it's never an issue to just absorb the dealings of people across situations and through stories.

Who knows?

Someday, we may take a leaf from that story and modify the learnings to suit ourselves.

Dunno about you all, but there have been instances quite a few where I have twisted and used the learnings from stories that my dad tells me. It is because of this reason, our dinner table conversations are always about life experiences and I particularly, end up taking a new lesson or so.

Every theory of management, be it modern business management or conventional management, and every principle of corporate governance or the governance of the country find some basis, some inspiration in our mythology.

Believe me, it would have been an honour to co-author this book with him – but as they say, the greatest actors cannot be the best directors or even writers – the same goes here.

So here I am, trying to put in a few learnings I have learnt from our fabled stories and incorporated in my business dealings and entrepreneurial life and hope it helps you in one manner or the other.

> ## Let Money Chase You

Again, this is not a rendition from the famous 3 Idiots movie dialogue about not chasing success – rather a learning from our past.

In Indian mythology, Lakshmi is the goddess of wealth. But there is a clear warning to its followers to not seek Lakshmi. Instead, they must make themselves more attractive to the goddess of wealth.

For that we have to be less like Indra, king of the gods, who is consumed by his own hunger, and more like Vishnu, preserver of the world, who is consumed by other people's hunger.

How does one do it?

Well, the answers is also written in there:

It says goddess Lakshmi, always follows Saraswati, the goddess of learning.

This simply means that if you have the right knowledge, wealth will follow you.

Now that's a vital shift for most businesses.

When I look back, I too had to make similar shifts.

In my naivety and earlier days, like all kids - I was chasing money.

Partly because of the mindset to earn fast, earn quick and earn more. I was hunting for deals to get that push towards financial success.

And not to mention, we you try something very very hard – you are bound to make mistakes.

This resulted in me getting depressed, anxious and a plethora of health disorders.

I gave up and took sometime to think with calmness and only when I shifted my focus from making money to myself; skills, personality, health, productivity, did I make money.

More precisely, money came to me.

Change yourself,

not the external.

So how does one make oneself attractive to wealth?

In the tales, the most priority was given to inner-prosperity. Only when your inner world was abundant, shall your outer world be so.

It means taking care of yourself, being healthy, and doing things that fill your soul.

Only then can you move to the external changes that may be learning new skills, investing in courses, etc.

› **Without Investment, there is No Return**

As I mentioned earlier, dinner table conversations in my house revolved around business logics and how one should do it.

This in a house, where I am the first-generation entrepreneur and that too a digital native one. Any which ways, it never hurts to listen.

Implementing or not on those criticisms and feedback is another game altogether.

So I have this mentor, who had this weird logic towards entrepreneurship – which states that he will not invest a penny, without an agreed foreseeable return.

As weird as it may sound, it is here where the mindset of an employee and an entrepreneur differs.

In Indian mythology, they have categorized two kinds of nature: Yajman (Someone, who makes a deal) & Asura (animal nature).

The yajaman is a social being:

the entrepreneur, the professional, the businessman, the promoter, the manufacturer, the service-provider who satisfies the hunger of a stakeholder, be it customer, employee, vendor, partner, boss or investor, in order to get what he wants.

Modern management has been today reduced to looking at business as a set of targets, or as a set of tasks. But business is essentially about a set of people who satisfy the hunger of the shareholder at one end and consumers at the other.

Don't be surprised if I inform you, that we all have embraced 'Asura' character or nature at some point in our business journey.

Let me explain and you will understand why my analogy says so:

So when I started Grazing Minds, my first B2C venture in 2018-19, I started out on social media platforms and focused on LinkedIn – as our audience was supposed to be learned and from professional world.

Nothing wrong in there.

I was hoping to get the same viral views I was getting on other social platforms, without offering anything to the readers of the platform.

The first few posts, we did was lacking research, effort and time – but were published just for the sake of presence.

However, I caught myself in the nick of time and decided to stick to a long-term approach, to cultivate the community by giving first.

Now, we ain't bothered about the LinkedIn algorithm or what it favours – in terms of kind of post or timing of post.

We educate our audience our view-points, irrespective of what's in-trend and the results amazed me.

I never spent a dollar on digital marketing or ads and got a purely organic engaging community from the globe just by sincere efforts.

So much, so that – we even got B2B leads from it.

You need to think of the areas in your business where you need to become like a Yajman (the giver). It's a sort of universal law, the more you give, the more you get.

But the question arises,

What can I give when I don't have anything?

This question is okay.

It's but natural for a struggling stressed-out individual, who barely makes enough money to pay bills.

That's when the first point comes into play.

You need to change yourself in such ways that you have more to give to the market.

More skills, more effort, more time.

Start giving content for free.

That's what I did through blogs, newsletters 10 years ago that built me a six-figure business – where I educated my B2B clients how travel has changed.

How money can be saved through usage of new tools and subtly introduce my tools and the cost-benefit analysis. So in a way, my readers turned to my potential customers.

But, for that to happen – they first need to be my readers – which can only happen, when I deliver value!

I don't think it's the problem of not having enough to give.

It's a question of your desire to give.

Even when writing content for free, we are writing it for our views. Not to help the reader.

We put the cart first, horse next.

Ourselves first, the customer next.

This won't get you or your cart anywhere. In 2014, when I was making content, I didn't get a response for six months. If I had put myself first, I would have quit right then.

> **Finding the key in Gita**

Call it cliché as you may, but no talk about Indian mythology and it's inspiration is incomplete without referring to Bhagavad Gita or Ramayana or any other Purana's.

Not getting into the spiritual aspect, but *The Bhagavad Gita* continues to be very relevant in the boardrooms of the 21st century across the world.

The Bhagavad Gita, also referred to as The Gita, comprises about 700 verses and is part of the ancient Indian classic, The Mahabharata.

While The Mahabharata centers on the power struggle between two groups of royal cousins and their battle in Kurukshetra in North India, The Gita is a conversation between two of its main characters, Arjuna and his mentor Krishna, in the battlefield.

Faced with the dilemma of waging war against his kin, Arjuna is paralyzed into inaction and turns to Krishna for counsel.

Responding to Arjuna's confusion, Krishna explains to Arjuna his duties as a warrior and a prince and also expounds on a range of practical and philosophical issues.

The setting of The Gita, in the midst of a battle, is widely considered as an allegory for the ethical and moral struggles of human life.

In my opinion, the idea of The Gita is fundamentally a global idea. It just happens that it originated in India.

Now why do I co-relate the learnings from Gita to corporate world,

Well, today's Kurukshetra is a corporate battle.

Anybody who is in a leadership role today is shaped by his or her history and culture and in turn also recreates a new process.

It's not an either/or process.

Someone who evolves out of a certain milieu carries the nuances of that milieu or that culture and, in turn, he will trans-create, he will impact the culture.

This can be mostly witnessed in family businesses or generational businesses, where you find hints of culture being passed on from each generation of leaders which is embodiment of the present working culture.

If you were to abandon those cultures, the whole business simply falls like a house of cards!

The modern (Western) management concepts of vision, leadership, motivation, excellence in work, achieving goals, giving work meaning, decision making and planning, are all discussed in the Bhagavad Gita.

There is one major difference.

While Western management thought too often deals with problems at material, external and peripheral levels, the Bhagavad Gita tackles the issues from the grass roots level of human thinking.

Once the basic thinking of man is improved, it will automatically enhance the quality of his actions and their results.

The problem with the management philosophy emanating from the West is that, while huge funds have been invested in building temples of modem management education, no perceptible changes are visible in the improvement of the general quality of life - although the standard of living of a few has gone up.

The same old struggles in almost all sectors of the economy: criminalization of institutions, social violence, exploitation and other vices are seen deep in the body politic.

This is because, the western idea of management centers on making the worker (and the manager) more efficient and more productive.

Companies offer workers more to work more, produce more, sell more and to stick to the organization without looking for alternatives.

The sole aim of extracting better and more work from the worker is to improve the bottom-line of the enterprise. The worker has become a hirable commodity, which can be used, replaced and discarded at will.

The western philosophy may have created prosperity for some people some of the time at least - but it has failed in the aim of ensuring betterment of individual life and social welfare. It has remained by and large a soulless edifice and an oasis of plenty for a few in the midst of poor quality of life for many.

Hence, there is an urgent need to re-examine prevailing management disciplines - their objectives, scope and content. Management should be redefined to underline the development of the worker as a person, as a human being, and not as a mere wage-earner. With this changed perspective, management can become an instrument in the process of social, and indeed national, development.

Now let us re-examine some of the modern management concepts in the light of the Bhagavad Gita which is a primer of management-by-values.

- **Utilization of available resources**

The first lesson of management science is to choose wisely and utilize scarce resources optimally. During the curtain raiser before the Mahabharata War, Duryodhana chose Sri Krishna's large army for his help while Arjuna selected Sri Krishna's wisdom for his support. This episode gives us a clue as to the nature of the effective manager - the former chose numbers, the latter, wisdom.

- Work commitment

A popular verse of the Gita advises "detachment" from the fruits or results of actions performed in the course of one's duty. Being dedicated work has to mean "working for the sake of work, generating excellence for its own sake." If we are always calculating the date of promotion or the rate of commission before putting in our efforts, then such work is not detached. It is not "generating excellence for its own sake" but working only for the extrinsic reward that may (or may not) result.

Working only with an eye to the anticipated benefits, means that the quality of performance of the current job or duty suffers - through mental agitation of anxiety for the future. In fact, the way the world works means that events do not always respond positively to our calculations and hence expected fruits may not always be forthcoming. So, the Gita tells us not to mortgage present commitment to an uncertain future.

Some people might argue that not seeking the business result of work and actions, makes one unaccountable. In fact, the Bhagavad Gita is full of advice on the theory of cause and effect, making the doer responsible for the consequences of his deeds. While advising detachment from the avarice of selfish gains in discharging one's accepted duty, the Gita does not absolve anybody of the consequences arising from discharge of his or her responsibilities.

Thus the best means of effective performance management is the work itself. Attaining this state of mind (called "nishkama karma") is the right attitude to work because it prevents the ego, the mind, from dissipation of attention through speculation on future gains or losses.

- Motivation self and self-transcendence

It has been presumed for many years that satisfying lower order needs of workers - adequate food, clothing and shelter, etc. are key factors in motivation. However, it is a common experience that the dissatisfaction of the clerk and of the Director is identical - only their scales and composition vary. It should be true that once the lower-order needs are more than satisfied, the Director should have little problem in optimizing his contribution to the organization and society.

But more often than not, it does not happen like that. ("The eagle soars high but keeps its eyes firmly fixed on the dead animal below.") On the contrary, a lowly paid schoolteacher, or a self-employed artisan, may well demonstrate higher levels of self-actualization despite poorer satisfaction of their lower-order needs.

This situation is explained by the theory of self-transcendence propounded in the Gita.

Self-transcendence involves renouncing egoism, putting others before oneself, emphasizing team work, dignity, co-operation, harmony and trust and indeed potentially sacrificing lower needs for higher goals, the opposite of Maslow.

- In conclusion

The despondency of Arjuna in the first chapter of the Gita is typically human. Sri Krishna, by sheer power of his inspiring words, changes Arjuna's mind from a state of inertia to one of righteous action, from the state of what the French philosophers call "anomie" or even alienation, to a state of self-confidence in the ultimate victory of "dharma" (ethical action.)

When Arjuna got over his despondency and stood ready to fight, Sri Krishna reminded him of the purpose of his new-found spirit of intense action - not for his own benefit, not for satisfying his own greed and desire, but for the good of many, with faith in the ultimate victory of ethics over unethical actions and of truth over untruth.

Sri Krishna's advice with regard to temporary failures is, "No doer of good ever ends in misery." Every action should produce results. Good action produces good results and evil begets nothing but evil. Therefore, always act well and be rewarded.

My purport is not to suggest discarding of the Western model of efficiency, dynamism and striving for excellence but to tune these ideals to India's holistic attitude of " lokasangraha" - for the welfare of many, for the good of many. There is indeed a moral dimension to business life. What we do in business is no different, in this regard, to what we do in our personal lives. The means do not justify the ends. Pursuit of results for their own sake, is ultimately self-defeating.

If anybody wants to do business in India or S.E.Asia, they have to study The Gita because most Indian CEOs swear by the book.

This and more will follow in the last part of the series.

Remember, *Mythology does more than provide literary entertainment; it also provides practical lessons to improve business performance!*

All the best.

~ AD

???

Page intentionally left blank

Acknowledgements

This book is especially significant to me as it brings together over fourteen years of research, experience and writing on a topic that's been very close to my heart and something I have been living day and night. It was also written during a period of the famous pandemic, where we were all locked up in our houses and we had to face tough days. Everyone, even the strongest person or leader on earth I know, had days of feeling low. When your business suffers, or your closed associates, loved one's are fighting the virus or sometimes lose their fight, it's but natural to have a feeling of being lost. I am fortunate to have met so many interesting and inspiring people along my journey. Those who mean a lot to me know who they are and how grateful I am for what they give me.

Also a debt of gratitude to my family, friends and relatives, who have always stood close to me in whatever I have done till date __ (the wackiest of business ideas or the unconventional marketing logics that I have implemented.)

Writing has been a part of my bucket list from school and college days and couldn't get time due to business commitments. However, I am grateful to the few important analytical souls in my life, who laughed at the idea of me writing books. (Seriously, they try to limit whenever you want to do something and they exist in my life too). So had you guys been not there, I wouldn't be propelled to do this – my inspiration!!

And finally, a bow of gratitude to the readers of my blogs, posts and the series I of the book – Insights from a shy entrepreneur along with it's podcast who have validated the importance of this work. You have made the effort worth it, many times over, and without you there would be no new edition.

Page intentionally left blank

Contact Information

To learn more, send an email to dash.asish@hotmail.com.

Engage with Asish by becoming part of his community by connecting with him on Linkedin https://in.linkedin.com/in/dashasish

Or

on twitter @dashasish (Asish Dash).

Alternatively you can connect down through any of his official mail ids and companies (Currently working on Grazing Minds)

Page intentionally left blank

Did you love *Insights from a Shy Entrepreneur : Turning Slowdown into Opportunity*? Then you should read *Insights From A Shy Entrepreneur*[1] by ASISH DASH!

Shy Entrepreneur Series : Volume -1

We have always been in awe of people who are successful and lead from the front.

However you will often find that, we individually have to make a continuous conscious effort in developing our skill set, by exploring resources available. There is no set course or book out there that can make you a complete leader. So much for the over-hyped and super-expensive MBA programs that just advertise their placement numbers and salaries offered and don't really focus on skills.

This series of books will touch on some aspects that help you decode your weaknesses and give an alternative way of developing a mindset, a way of re-engineering your perception to problem solving to make you a more effective leader.It also uses the B.E.S.T. approach to leadership and certain other subtle processes that help you become a better leader and an entrepreneur.

Read more at https://in.linkedin.com/in/dashasish.

Also by ASISH DASH

The Shy Entrepreneur
Insights From A Shy Entrepreneur
Insights from a Shy Entrepreneur : Turning Slowdown into Opportunity

Watch for more at https://in.linkedin.com/in/dashasish.

About the Author

Asish Dash, is the Founder of Grazing Minds - the fastest growing sustainable consulting edtech platform.

Asish defines himself as 3E. (Engineer, Economist and Entrepreneur) an alumnus of world's Top 10 university and various other institutes.

Frugality in business, is his passion and so is creating low cost self sustaining business models.He loves talking, studying and decoding business models and innovation around it.

After 3 successful startups, He is all into sharing information. He believes writing books is one way in which he can connect to my audiences apart from the consulting he does on LinkedIn.

Though some of his opinions may be termed as brash and opinionated - but he says, he is not here to appease any corporations or lobbies!!

Read more at https://in.linkedin.com/in/dashasish.

CPSIA information can be obtained
at www.ICGtesting.com
Printed in the USA
BVHW051547090822
644144BV00007B/383